Doctors and Company: A Dictionary of Health
Care Givers

Doctors and Company: A Dictionary of Health Care Givers

By

Rosemarie Riechel

ISBN 1-58500-620-3

1stBooks - rev. 01/20/00

About the Book

The complex workings of the human body are explored in many books that define and explain human anatomy. But many people have problems finding answers to questions about the complicated world of medical specialists and other healthcare givers. How can the need for this information be met? *Doctors and Company: A Dictionary of Healthcare Givers* provides concise, easily understood definitions that clear up the confusion about what various medical specialists, nurses, dentists, alternative medicine practitioners, and other professionals do. This book provides information on choosing a doctor and dentist, and on alternative medicine. It includes a subject list of doctors and other health care givers and a selected bibliography. In addition, the phonetic pronunciation for each entry is provided and definitions of medical terms appear throughout the text. *Doctors and Company* is a quick reference source for anyone in need of uncomplicated answers about the health care community.

Contents

Introduction

Many years ago the family doctor would care for everyone, from baby to grandparents. The doctor would know everyone's medical history, treat routine illnesses, do minor surgery, give vaccinations, and teach patients how to stay well. Today family practice has evolved into a fairly new specialty. After completing a training program in various aspects of internal medicine, minor surgery, obstetrics, gynecology, orthopaedics, pediatrics, geriatric care, and preventive medicine, the doctor becomes board certified.

Any doctor may limit practice to a particular specialty after receiving an M.D. degree and a license to practice medicine. But, without the additional two to three year training program and examination (approved by a member board of the American Board of Medical Specialists) to achieve diplomate status, the doctor is not a bonafide specialist. Going one step further, a fellowship is awarded to a doctor who participates in an additional training and certification program in research and clinical methodology that focuses on a narrower aspect of a specific area of specialization--a subspecialty. For example, diagnostic laboratory immunology is a subspecialty of allergy and immunology.

In this age of specialties and subspecialties, learning about all the different kinds of doctors seems daunting. The baby is taken to the pediatrician. A teenager may visit an adolescent medical specialist and also be treated for drug addiction by an adolescent psychiatrist. A sister or brother with hayfever will visit an allergist. Your mother will see her gynecologist. Father will go to a gastroenterologist to get relief from his constant indigestion. Grandmother and grandfather will be cared for by a geriatrician, while visiting a geriatric psychiatrist to treat depression, or an audiologist to be fitted for a hearing aid.

To compound the confusion, there are more than fifteen different doctors that specialize in treating the diseases and disorders of children. Also, in order to discover the cause of your health problem, you may be referred to a number of different specialists trained in new technologies and new methods of diagnosis within their fields of expertise.

Do you know why you are sent to various different doctors?

Do you know the difference between a psychiatrist and a physiatrist, who sound similar but have very different specialties? Do you know the difference between an ophthalmologist and an optometrist, whose practices are similar? Why does your dentist send you to a periodontist or prosthodontist? Do you know that there is no difference in education and training between a Doctor of Medical Dentistry (D.M.D.) and a Doctor of Dental Surgery (D.D.S.)?

Turning to alternative medical practitioners, do you know what chiropractors, acupuncturists, or touch therapists do? What is the difference between alternative medical practitioners and traditional health care providers?

In these days of an increasingly complex medical community, it is important to understand what different health care professionals do in order to fully comprehend what specific roles they have in your, or your family's health care.

Once the confusion about who does what and why is eliminated, you can understand the diagnosis and treatment process better, and ask appropriate questions of each health care giver you encounter.

This dictionary is designed as an easy-to-use reference book that will help you find out about the professionals who research, diagnose, treat and prevent illness. It is arranged alphabetically and includes a listing by subject.

A pronounciation guide appears in brackets after each entry.

The meanings of some medical words are included in the text, eliminating the need to flip to a glossary.

If you need information on health, medicine, and the human body, a selected bibliography is included to get you started.

While not all-inclusive, this dictionary answers questions about many health care professionals. You will gain a better understanding of why you are referred to them, and what role each one plays in the treatment of specific illnesses and disorders. It is a practical reference guide to major health care professionals who treat our complicated bodies and complex minds in order to make us feel better and keep us well.

Choosing a Doctor and Dentist

Choosing a doctor who has both skill and compassion is difficult. Some people go about finding the best doctor by asking for recommendations from family members, friends, and neighbors. Others contact a medical society or hospital to obtain names of doctors near to where they live, or ask a trusted family practitioner for referrals to specialists. Answering a doctor's community newspaper or newsletter advertisement, or selecting a doctor from the telephone directory are the most inefficient methods of locating the best practitioner for you.

Any recommendation rarely includes information about background, expertise, personality, or practice. This information can be found in the *Official ABMS Directory of Board Certified Medical Specialists*, available in most public libraries. The doctors are listed alphabetically by specific geographical area within each specialty. Each entry includes certification and recertification dates for the specialty and/or subspecialty, birth date and place of birth, medical school attended and graduation date, internship, residency, fellowship dates and places, dates and locations of hospital and academic appointments, professional memberships, type of practice, and office address, telephone, and fax numbers.

This multivolume directory also has a list of certification codes, other codes and abbreviations, national and sectional societies, a list of United States and Canadian accredited medical schools (with address, telephone number, and dean's name), a list of state licensing boards (including address, telephone number and contact person's name), the history and development of the American Board of Medical Specialties, its mission statement, information on the process of certification and recertification, a list of approved specialty boards, descriptions of all recognized specialties and subspecialties, and certification and recertification requirements,

Why is all this so important? Knowledge of a doctor's background and credentials tells you what the extent of the doctor's training and experience is, and whether or not he or she is a vital, active, committed practitioner.

Even though a doctor's credentials are impressive, he or she may fall short of excellence in patient care, communication skills, compassion, attentiveness, dedication, charm and availability. Whether or not the doctor you choose meets your needs for best doctor can only be verified by an office visit. Does the doctor take an extensive medical history? Does he or she listen to your questions and concerns and take the time to answer, discuss your health problems, explain treatment options and test procedures, the need for certain medications and their possible side effects? Does he or she talk to you about preventive methods for maintaining health and wellness care? Does the doctor make you feel like a whole person, rather than a specimen? Are you invited to telephone if you have any problems or questions?

Doctor's who recognize the importance of working with their patients know that the success of their care and treatment depends on a healthy and productive doctor-patient relationship.

Although new technology has made a visit to the dentist less stressful, the fear of pain and the usually high out-of-pocket costs makes finding a practitioner you trust and feel totally comfortable with very important. Your search for the best dentist available should be more than just asking a friend for a recommendation, checking the telephone book, or answering an advertisement that promises fast and painless treatment of all dental problems in a single office.

Choosing a dentist who practices in his or her own small office has the advantage of a close patient-doctor relationship that can be so comforting. But no dentist is an expert in all aspects of the profession, so you can expect to be referred to a specialist for complex problems such as gum disease, root canal work, or extraction.

Group practices with two or more dentists sharing the same office have the benefits of longer hours, availability for emergencies, on-premises laboratories, specialists on staff, and immediate consultation for difficult problems. But if a large group practice emphasizes patient volume and profit, the quality of treatment becomes doubtful.

As with medical doctors, it is important to check the dentist's credentials--education, specialty training, board certification, and type of practice.

Are you aware of the training requirements beyond the dental degree needed to become board certified in one of the dental specialties? To qualify, the dentist is required to take an additional two year course of study in an accredited dental school to receive certification from a certification organization recognized by the American Dental Association (ADA).

The *American Dental Directory* has an alphabetical index of dentists practicing in the United States. Arranged by state, each entry includes the dentist's address, year of birth, ADA membership status, specialty, dental school code, year of graduation, whether the dentist is a diplomate certified by a recognized specialty board, whether he or she is licensed by the state licensing board, whether American Dental Association accredited educational programs were completed, and if the dentist is in general practice or if the practice is limited to a particular specialty.

This information, together with an office visit to meet the dentist and the staff of hygienists and technicians, as well as to check out the equipment (the latest should be in use), will help you choose a dentist committed to giving you the best care.

Considering Alternative Medicine

The wide range of diagnostic approaches and treatment methods offered by alternative medicine practitioners is attractive to many people for a variety of reasons:

Many people lose faith in scientific medicine because no "magic" bullet exists to cure such devastating diseases as drug resistant tuberculosis, cancer, AIDS, cystic fibrosis, and coronary defects.

The cost of health care and medical insurance is too high to be affordable--especially for catastrophic illnesses and chronic diseases.

Many people are deprived of good health care because they have no health insurance. Insurance is not an issue for alternative medicine practitioners.

Quality care and freedom to choose, especially when you

belong to an HMO, is often not an option or too restrictive. Alternative medicine, on the other hand, allows you to take charge of your own health care.

Drugs and surgery (and their side effects) can be scary and risky. Alternative treatments sound simpler, safer, and painless.

Many people believe that alternative medicine might be the key to curing a terminal illness, since practitioners provide you with a (false) optimism that medical science cannot.

Even though the term *alternative medicine* embraces a variety of different approaches to healing and maintaining health, all of them have certain beliefs in common:

The human body has the power to heal itself, so the practitioners focus on stimulating the body (with proper diet, herbal medicines, nutritional supplements, massage, manipulation, for example) to speed up the healing process.

Your lifestyle, human relationships, societal and

environmental influences, view of personal self-worth within the human community, and your perception of yourself influences your state of health or illness.

The interrelationship of mind and body is essential to health. Thoughts, emotions, feelings, and attitudes are thought to have a direct effect on physical health or illness.

Your spiritual life and religious beliefs are most important to your state of wellness. Alternative medicine practitioners believe that faith alone can bring about cures, and belief in a treatment can influence its success.

Alternative treatments are thought to be safe because they are non-invasive-- lifestyle changes, developing a positive attitude toward your body, mind, and spirit, doing relaxation exercises and meditation to gain harmony within yourself and with the cosmos, using diet and exercise to balance energy and your life force.

Symptoms of illness or disease are not treated. Rather, the treatment is holistic (care of the entire patient--mind and body), since any illness, disease or disorder is believed to be the result of a complex imbalance of the physical, emotional, mental, spiritual, social, and philosophical elements of each individual.

All body systems are as interrelated as each person is to society, the environment, and the universe. Alternative treatments are used to balance these interrelationships.

Energy, or the vital force, must flow easily to maintain balance. If a part of the system is out of balance, treatment will release the energy blockage and restore harmony to the whole.

Natural substances from plants, and sometimes mineral and animal sources, are thought to be superior to drugs and other medicines and therapies used by medical doctors. Alternative practitioners reason that they are elements of nature and produce fewer side effects.

Some alternative treatments and herbal remedies have been accepted by the medical community because controlled, scientific studies have proven their (limited) effectiveness. The manipulation techniques of chiropractic (now widely accepted by medical insurance companies for specific uses), as well as acupuncture, relaxation excercises, and meditation are examples of these alternative treatments.

Treatments commonly used in physical and rehabilitation medicine are alternative methods now recognized and successfully used by medical doctors. They focus on the whole person (mind and body) and manual healing and health maintenance through correct body movement, improved posture, joint mobility, balance, cardiopulmonary function, consistent exercise, transcutaneous electrical nerve stimulation, heat, ice, traction (to control pain), and on improving occupational skills function.

How are alternative medicine treatments proven effective by the medical community? The National Institutes of Health, Office of Alternative Medicine (OAM) is responsible for promoting unbiased scientific study of alternative therapies that are thought to have the potential of improving health and maintaining wellness. The OAM sponsors investigation and research into alternative treatments, provides educational and training programs on evaluatory methods, and provides accurate and current information on all aspects of alternative medicine to researchers, doctors, and the general public.

All alternative medicine practices are labelled quackery by those who believe that scientific medicine is the only medical profession. In fact, it may surprise you to learn that back in the 1960's the American Medical Association denounced chiropractic as fraudulent.

Unfortunately, the lure of the magic cure-all, the miracle elixir, the mysterious treatment that can restore health, eliminate all disease, and cure chronic and terminal illnesses, has allowed quackery to thrive. The winners are the charlatans with no skills other than that for making a profit, medical doctors gone astray, and other misguided health care professionals.

Quacks are hard to identify, especially by people looking for that "magic bullet" that promises recovery and restored health. Some signs of fraud and quackery are listed below.

Loud condemnation of modern medicine is meant to shake your faith in scientifically proven treatments--claiming they are toxic and useless. For example: radiation therapy kills your life force by poisoning your entire body; it is not necessary to treat diabetes with insulin if you follow the right diet; raw milk is healthier than pasturized milk; silver amalgam dental fillings should be replaced because they are toxic.

Some medical doctors use their credentials to hawk books with questionable health advice, along with dangerous diets and health care products that guarantee cures.

The media is used to get wide publicity for rapidly churned out books that are variations on the benefits of the same alternative therapies--making false claims about how to get healthy, avoid aging, cure chronic ailments, and experience remission and freedom from potentially fatal diseases. The treatments recommended include exercise regimens, exotic diets, lifestyle changes, meditation, and various herbal mixtures.

If an alternative practitioner claims that you can be healed from miles away by mental powers or cosmic vibrations you are dealing with a quack. You usually have to purchase a high-priced useless device like a magical black box so the medium can start the cure.

Any health product catalog that advertises magical potions, creams, miracle teas, and nutritional supplements that are guaranteed to work should be ignored.

Alternative practitioners who use frequent x-rays to "diagnose" your problem and "keep track" of the healing process are dangerous to your health and wallet. The need for frequent visits (at a high cost) is stressed in order to successfully "cure" your disorder and maintain health.

If a chiropractor, or other alternative medicine practitioner, claims that manipulation and massage can cure tuberculosis, diabetes, cancer, AIDS, heart disease, mumps, pneumonia, allergies, sore throat, inflammatory bowel disease, and more, you have found the ultimate quack.

The person who claims that organic food and natural vitamins are superior to other foods and better for your health is falsely advertising high priced produce and products for personal gain.

The best way to weed out quackery is by carefully and objectively scrutinizing alternative practitioners and their methods of treatment. Here are some guidelines to follow:

Discuss all alternative treatments and remedies you are considering with your doctor. The therapies may be harmful and the remedies you take may cause dangerous side effects, especially when taken with particular prescription drugs.

Contact the appropriate health care association, or the Office of Alternative Medicine for information on the validity of a treatment and background on the practitioner.

Since the treatment will most likely not be covered by health insurance, consider the cost.

Do not rely on testimonials and personal accounts of miracle cures offered by the practitioner, or in advertisements. They are not proof that the treatment really works.

Find out about the history and development of particular alternative practices. Read books and other publications written by both alternative medicine practioners and medical doctors and compare what is said about the safety and validity of particular treatments.

Through open-minded, unbiased examination of alternative methods and their potential for preventing and treating illness, you will be able to make informed decisions about your health care, while recognizing the scams and discarding the quackery.

The Doctors and Other Health Care Givers

Abdominal surgeon.

(ab-dom'-i-nl sur'-jun)

An abdominal surgeon performs surgery on the abdominal organs (stomach, intestines, liver, spleen, gall bladder, pancreas, uterus, and appendix).

Acupuncturist.

(ack'-you-punk'-chur-ist)

A person who practices the ancient Chinese medical procedure that treats illness, relieves pain, or locally anesthetises the body (make it insensitive to pain) by piercing the skin with fine needles at specific sites of the body where pain centers are located.

Adolescent medicine specialist.

(ad-oh-les'-ent med'-i-sin spesh'-uh-list)

A doctor who specializes in the health needs and problems of adolescents, this specialist studies, diagnoses, and treats disorders and diseases, and provides preventive care such as checkups and vaccinations.

Adolescent psychiatrist.

(ad-oh-les'-ent sy-ky'-eh-trist)

An adolescent psychiatrist specializes in the study, diagnosis, treatment, and prevention of adolescent mental illness, emotional disorders, or addictions to drugs or other substances with psychoanalysis, prescription drugs, or both.

Adult nurse practitioner.

(ah-dult' nurs prak-tish'-uh-ner)

A registered nurse with special training in caring for ill or infirm (weak, feeble) adults. This person is qualified to diagnose and treat minor physical disorders and chronic illnesses.

Allergist.

(al'-er-gist)

An allergist specializes in the diagnosis and treatment of disorders that cause the immune system (the system that protects the body from organisms that cause disease) to overreact to ordinarily harmless substances such as dust, tree and grass pollen, certain odors, and foods.

Anesthesiologist.

(an-iss-thee'-zee-ahl'-oh-jist)

An anesthesiologist administers both local and general anesthesia (drugs that cause the loss of the abilility to feel pain), and monitors a patient's vital signs during and after surgery, an obstetric (childbirth), or diagnostic procedure (a method of analysing or finding disease). This specialist also diagnoses and treats patients with acute (severe) and long-lasting pain, people who are critically ill, and those with severe injuries, cardiac (heart), and respiratory (breathing) emergencies.

Anesthetist.

(a-nes'-thi-tist)

This person administers anesthetics for diagnostic procedures or surgery. An anesthetist is either a specially trained nurse or technician.

Alternative medicine practitioner.

(awl-ter'-na-tiv med'-i-sin prak-tish'-uh-ner)

This person uses one or more of a variety of well-known or exotic treatments that focus on stimulating the body (through diet, herbal medicines, nutritional supplements, massage, or manipulation, for example) to heal illness or disorders. The interrelationship of mind and body is as essential to successful treatment as is lifestyle, human relationships, societal and environmental influences, and an individual's perception of self and self-worth. Non-invasive treatments, such as lifestyle changes, developing a positive attitude toward one's body, mind, and spirit, relaxation, and meditation, natural substances rather than drugs, diet, and exercise are believed to be both safe and effective. Although the medical community dismisses most of the cures claimed by alternative practitioners, some techniques, such as chiropractic and acupuncture, are accepted for certain medical problems.

Aromatherapist.

(ah-roh'-ma-ther'-uh-pist)

Aromatherapists use natural essential oils from a variety of aromatic plants to cure a person's ills. They believe that the oils have therapeutic powers that balance the spirit, mind, and body because of the link between the sense of smell and memory. Treatments include massage, inhalation, and baths to relieve pain, muscle spasm, headache, poor appetite, respiratory and circulatory problems, and any other stress-related conditions. Aromatherapy is sometimes used along with chiropractic, reflexology, and dietary adjustment. Aromatherapy is not an approved treatment, since it has not been proven effective by the medical community.

Audiologist.

(aw-dee-ahl'-oh-jist)

An audiologist is licensed to test and evaluate hearing ability and to treat people with hearing impairment (hearing loss) with hearing aids.

Cardiologist.

(car-dee-ahl'-oh-jist)

The cardiologist studies, diagnoses, and treats such heart diseases as abnormal heart beat, heart attack (sudden lack of enough oxygen to supply the heart, causing heart muscle damage), congestive heart failure (the heart pumps insufficient amounts of blood), and congenital (since birth) heart defects.

Cardiovascular surgeon.

(kahr-dee-oh-vas'-kyu-luhr sur'-jun)

A cardiovascular surgeon performs surgery on the heart and blood vessels, and performs open heart surgery and heart transplants.

Certified nurse-midwife.

(sir-tif'-eyed nurs mid'-weif)

A certified nurse-midwife is a registered nurse with special training in the care of pregnant women and in assisting them in childbirth. This person also decides when a medical doctor should be called.

Chelation therapist.

(kee-lay'-shun ther'-uh-pist)

A chelation (from the Greek *chele*--claw) therapist uses EDTA (ethylene diamine tetraacetic acid), a synthetic amino acid that claws, or binds itself to heavy toxic metals in the body when it is slowly fed into the body intravenously. Medical doctors use EDTA chelation for treating poisoning by lead, mercury, cadmium, iron, and other toxic metals. Chelation is also used for such unproven and unapproved treatments as high blood pressure, coronary artery disease, arteriosclerosis (loss of elasticity and blood flow in vessel walls due to thickening of the vessel walls, as well as deposits of calcium), angina (severe, constricting pain usually caused by coronary artery disease), rheumatoid arthritis, multiple sclerosis, muscular dystrophy, cancer, and other chronic, life-threatening diseases.

Child psychiatrist.

(chyld sy-ky'-ah-trist)

This doctor specializes in the diagnosis, treatment, and prevention of mental illnesses, emotional disorders, and addictions of children, treating them with psychoanalysis, prescription drugs, or both.

Child psychologist.

(chyld sy-kol'-oh-jist)

A child psychologist is a licensed professional who specializes in the science of the child's mind and how it works. This person analyzes, and treats children with mental and emotional problems using counseling therapy. A child psychologist cannot prescribe drugs.

Chiropodist.

(ky-rop'-oh-dist)

Also called a podiatrist (puh-dy'-uh-trist),this professional is licensed to diagnose and treat foot disorders, such as bunions (inflamation and enlargement of the big toe joint), calluses (a hardened and thickened part of the skin), corns (a rough growth of tissue with a sensitive core that forms over a bone because of friction or pressure), and tendon (connective tissue like a cord that fastens the ends of muscle to bone) inflamations.

Chiropractor.

(ky'-ro-prak-tor)

A chiropractor treats disorders of the skeletal and nervous systems and restores and maintains a patient's health by manipulating (adjusting) the spinal vertebrae (the bones that make up the backbone, or spine) and joints (where bones meet). Some chiropractors also use acupressure (finger pressure to rub, or massage specific body sites), exercise, body massage, the application of heat and cold, and dietary changes.

Clinical and laboratory immunology specialist.

(klin'-i-kal and lab'-ruh-tor-ee im-yuh-nol'-uh-jee spesh'-uh-list)

This doctor specializes in the diagnosis and treatment of disorders resulting from abnormal immune system responses by conducting laboratory tests and other procedures.

Clinical ecology practitioner.

(klin'-i-kal i-kol'-oh-jee praktish'-uh-ner)

This person's treatment method originated with the study of food allergies as the cause of such medical problems as asthma, colitis, arthritis, depression, anxiety, fatigue, and migraine headache. Exposure to hundreds of contaminants in the environment (chemicals, pesticides, automobile exhaust, chemical ingredients in industrial and houshold products) are believed to cause health problems like mood disorders, fatigue, abdominal, urinary, circulatory problems, palpitations, arthritis, respiratory illness, and psychosis. This person diagnoses a problem by using a test called "Provocation and Neutralization." The suspected offending substance is either injected under the skin or given under the tongue to provoke a reaction. The treatment consists of avoiding the toxic substances, living and working in a controlled environment, taking nutritional substances, inhaling pure oxygen, or drinking urine. Although the medical community has proven the theory that environmental pollutants do affect overall health, the non-standard diagnostic and treatment methods used invalidate clinical ecology as a medical discipline.

Colon and rectal surgeon.

(ko'-lon and rek'-tul sur'-jun)

Also known as a proctologist (prok-tol'-uh-jist), this doctor diagnoses and surgically treats diseases of the colon (the main part of the large intestine), the rectum (the last part of the large intestine that holds the feces), the anal canal (from the rectum to the anus), and the anus (the opening through which the feces (waste matter) passes. Examples of the diseases treated are hemorrhoids (varicose veins in the anus area), fissures (openings caused by splits in the tissue), diverticulitis (inflamation of a sac-like abnormality in the colon), and cancer.

Critical care specialist.

(krit'-i-kal kair spesh'-uh-list)

This specialist diagnoses and treats patients with a life-threatening illness in an intensive care unit (ICU) of a hospital. These illnesses include heart attack (sudden lack of enough oxygen to supply the heart, causing heart muscle damage), heart failure (heart stops pumping leading to death, or the heart does not pump enough blood), stroke (a blockage or hemorrhage of a blood vessel leading to the brain), shock, drug overdose, or multiple injuries.

Critical care surgeon.

(krit'-i-cal kair sur'-jun)

A critical care surgeon provides immediate treatment to patients with a life-threatening condition by performing a surgical procedure (operation).

Dental hygienist.

(den'-tl hi-jen'-ist)

A dental hygienist is trained and licensed to clean teeth, take dental x-rays, and perform other tasks under the supervision of a dentist.

Dental technician.

(den'-tl tek-nish'-en)

A dental technician makes bridges and dentures according to the instructions of the dentist.

Dentist—general dentistry.

(den'-tist--jen'-er-al den'-tis-tree)

A dentist in general practice treats tooth and gum problems, fills cavities, pulls teeth, repairs decayed or damaged teeth with crowns, caps, bridges, and performs cosmetic procedures like bleaching, bonding, and reshaping broken or malformed teeth. A general dentist treats children and adults, and refers patients to dental specialists. Some dentists have D.D.S (doctor of dental surgery) after their names, while others use D.M.D. (doctor of medical dentistry). There is no difference in the training they receive in dental school.

Dermatologist.

(dur-ma-tol'-oh-jist)

A dermatologist diagnoses and treats children, adolescents, and adults with benign (not cancerous) or malignant (cancerous) disorders of the skin, mouth, hair, and nails. Some disorders are skin cancer, moles (small, elevated dark spot on the skin), melanomas (skin tumors), contact dermatitis (inflamation caused by touch), and scars. Treatments include medicines, surgery, electrosurgery, laser, or grafts.

Emergency medicine specialist.

(ee-mur'-jen-see med'-i-sin spesh'-uh-list)

This doctor immediately diagnoses and treats patients with severe illness or trauma (a body wound or shock caused by physical injury), and other medical emergencies in a hospital emergency room (ER).

Endocrinologist.

(en-doh-kri-nol'-oh-jist)

An endocrinologist studies, diagnoses, and treats disorders of the endocrine glands, which include the pineal gland, thyroid gland, the parathyroids, thymus, adrenal glands, pancreas, the testes in men, and the ovaries in women. These glands release chemicals (called hormones) directly into the blood to regulate growth, metabolism (the chemical processes that break down substances to release energy needed to live and build up substances needed by the body), and sexual development and functioning.

Endodontist.

(en-doh-don'-tist)

An endodontist is a dentist who specializes in the diagnosis, prevention, and treatment of the dental pulp (the soft tissue inside a tooth) by removing the nerve and pulp cavity tissue and filling it. This treatment is called root canal therapy.

Family nurse practitioner.

(fam'-i-lee nurs prak-tish'-uh-ner)

This registered nurse has special training in the care of patients of all ages within a family unit.

Family physician.

(fam'-i-lee fi-zish'-en)

This doctor diagnoses and treats the diseases and disorders of individuals and their families, provides well-care, and teaches preventive medicine and health techniques to patients. Family practice includes all body systems, internal organs, diseases and disorders of patients of any age or sex. Referrals to specialists are made when the patient's health problem is more complex.

Gastroenterologist.

(gas'-troh-en'-ter-ahl'-uh-jist)

The gastroenterologist studies, diagnoses, and treats disorders of the digestive system (the esophagus, stomach, liver, intestinal tract, pancreas, and gallbladder). Some disorders are abdominal pain, chronic indigestion, ulcers, colitis (inflamation of the colon, or large intestine), diarrhea, and cancer.

General surgeon.

(jen'-eh-rahl sur'jun)

This specialist surgically treats a variety of disorders, diseases, and injuries occuring in almost any part of the body by performing operations. A general surgeon refers patients to a special surgeon when specific expertise is required.

Geriatric psychiatrist.

(jer-ee-at'-trik sy-ky'-eh-trist)

A geriatric psychiatrist specializes in the diagnosis, treatment, and prevention of mental illnesses, emotional disorders, and addictions of the elderly.

Geriatrician.

(jer-ee-uh-trish'-un)

This doctor specializes in the prevention, diagnosis, and treatment of disorders of the elderly such as incontinence (inability to control urination or bowel movements), injuries from falls, Parkinson's disease, and Alzheimer's disease.

Gynecologic oncologist.

(guy-neh-kol-loj'-i-kul on-kol'-oh-jist)

An oncologist who specializes in the diagnosis and treatment of cancers of the female reproductive system and genital tract.

Gynecologist.

(guy-neh-kol'-oh-jist)

A gynecologist diagnoses and medically and surgically treats disorders of the female reproductive organs.

Hand surgeon.

(hand sur'-jun)

This specialist diagnoses and treats hand and wrist disorders and injuries.

Head and neck surgeon.

(hed and nek sur'-jun)

A head and neck surgeon performs surgery on the head and the neck--excluding the eyes and the brain.

Hematologist.

(hee-mah-tol'-oh-jist)

A hematologist studies, diagnoses, and treats diseases of the blood, blood clotting, bone marrow, lymph glands, and spleen. These diseases include anemia, blood clotting disorders like hemophilia (much bleeding from minor injuries due to missing or abnormal clotting factor in the blood), leukemia (cancer of the bone marrow with increase of white blood cells in tissue), and sickle cell anemia (chronic hereditary blood disease in which red blood cells become sickle-shaped and nonfunctioning causing anemia, blood clotting, and joint pain).

Herbalist.

(ur'-bah-list)

The herbalist examines all elements of health or illness that influence well-being before prescribing an herb, or a mixture of herbs that will detoxify and eliminate impurities that cause disease, or develop as a result of disease. The herbs prescribed for each individual are supposed to maintain the body's health, allow healing, and prevent illness by strengthening the body's systems and maintaining energy balance. Diet, nutritional supplements (vitamins and minerals), relaxation techniques, exercise, and posture correction are commonly used together with the prescribed herbal remedies. Many of the drugs prescribed by doctors contain ingredients that come from plant matter, but herbal products are approved for sale as food supplements only. Diagnosis and treatment by herbalists is not recommended.

Homeopathist.

(hoh-me-op'-uh-thist)

A person who treats disease with minute doses of natural medicines from plant, mineral, and animal substances to stimulate the patient's ability to heal without suffering any harmful side effects as one might when taking chemical substances. A homeopathist believes that the same medicines that cause symptoms of a disease in healthy people would cure sick persons. For example, a runny eye symptom of hayfever or a cold would be treated with onion since it causes the eyes to run; nausea would be treated with ipecac (used to induce vomiting or bowel movements) because it makes a healthy person nauseous; lead poisoning would be treated with a miniscule amount of lead. Large doses of homeopathic remedies are believed to cause a worsening of symptoms, so doses are reduced to very tiny amounts so no side effects would occur. Medical doctors do not prescribe homeopathic remedies because such tiny doses of medicines are useless in fighting diseases and infections. Despite the homeopathist's belief, these remedies have not been scientifically proven to be effective.

Immunodermatologist.

(im'-yuh-noh-dur-ma-tol'-oh-jist)

This doctor studies the causes of and treats skin diseases that originate from a defective immune system. Diagnosis is done through analysis of tissue cells.

Immunologist.

(im-yuh-nol'-oh-jist)

An immunologist studies the immune system (the system that causes the body to resist infection), and how the body responds to infection. This specialist diagnoses and treats immune system disorders that are acquired (contracted) or congenital (existing at birth), immune system deficiency, and autoimmune disease (a faulty immune reaction that damages parts of the patient's body).

Infectious disease specialist.

(in-fek'-shus dih'-zeez spesh'-uh-list)

This doctor studies, diagnoses, and treats all types of infectious diseases that may be spread by direct physical contact, mucus droplets, or by animals or insects (racoons, mosquitoes, for example). An infectious disease specialist is an expert in preventive medicine and travel-related disorders.

Internist.

(in-tur'-nist)

An internist is an expert in diagnosing and treating disorders of the internal systems of the body, common disorders of the eyes, ears, nose, and throat, nervous, cardiovascular, and other body systems. This doctor might be a family practitioner, or specialize in diagnosing and treating disorders of a particular body system, such as the gastric, cardiovascular, or nervous systems.

Iridologist.

(ir'-i-dol'-uh-jist)

An iridologist believes that the eye (as part of the brain) receives impulses from every part of the body. Imbalances in organs, limbs, and other body systems can be diagnosed by studying the iris (the colored portion of the eye) and comparing what is seen to charts that relate the different parts of the body to various segments of the iris. An iridologist believes that various spots, lines and colors appear when the corresponding part of the body is out of balance. Only general disturbances (not specific diseases) can be detected. There is no evidence that iridology has any validity.

Licensed practical nurse.

(lie'-sensd prak'-ti-kal nurs)

A licensed practical nurse (LPN), trained in a vocational technical school, a community college, or a hospital program, provides general nursing care.

Maternal neonatal gynecological nurse.

(muh-tur'-nul nee-oh-nay'-tul guy-neh-ko-lah'-ji-kul nurs)

This nurse specialist cares for mothers and their newborn babies.

Medical geneticist.

(med'-ie-kul je-net'-uh-sist)

A medical geneticist specializes in the study of the genetic origins of inherited diseases and disorders and how they are transmitted. This doctor also determines the methods that should be used to prevent and control genetic (existing at birth) diseases.

Medical surgical nurse.

(med'-ie-kul sur'-ji-kul nurs)

A medical surgical nurse specializes in caring for patients before and after they have had surgery, and for adults with chronic (lasting for a long time) illnesses.

Naturopathist.

(nay'-chuh-rop-eh-thist)

Naturopathists believe in natural (drugless) healing that comes from the body's natural ability to cleanse itself of toxins (poisons that cause illness) and regain its harmony with nature. This person is convinced that health depends on living a natural and hygenic life. Air, light, water, natural foods, exercise and rest are thought to be essential to maintaining, or regaining health. Treatments include acupuncture, homeopathy, hydrotherapy (use of water), megavitamins, herbal teas, reflexology, chelation therapy, and natural foods. While there is some validity to the belief in living a clean life, the treatments could be quite risky.

Neonatal-perinatal medicine specialist:

(nee-oh-nay'-tul per'-ee-nay'-tul med'-i-sin spesh'-uh-list)

This doctor diagnoses and treats premature and sick newborn infants.

Nephrologist.

(neh-phrol'-uh-jist)

A nephrologist specializes in the diagnosis and treatment of kidney disorders, and treats patients with non-functioning kidneys with dialysis (a special machine that cleanses the circulating blood of uric acid and urea) and transplantation.

Neurologist.

(nuh-rol'-oh-jist)

This specialist studies, diagnoses, and medically treats disorders of the nervous system, brain, and spinal cord.

Neurosurgeon.

(noo-roh-sur'-jun)

A neurosurgeon studies, diagnoses, and surgically treats disorders of the nervous system, brain, and spinal cord.

Nuclear medicine specialist.

(noo'-klee-ur med'-i-sin spesh'-uh-list)

A nuclear medicine specialist is a doctor who is expert in using radioactive substances to diagnose and treat diseases like malignant (cancerous) and benign (non-cancerous) tumors and thyroid disorders.

Nurse practitioner.

(nurs prak-tish'-uh-nur)

This registered nurse is trained and certified to perform some of the functions of a medical doctor, limited to the diagnosis and treatment of some common minor ailments (illness or physical disorder).

Nutritionist.

(noo-trish'-uh-nist)

A nutritionist is qualified to teach people about nutrition and plan meals to meet an individual's health and dietary (the foods one eats) needs.

Obstetrician.

(ob-steh-trish'-un)

An obstetrician cares for women during pregnancy, childbirth, and after delivery.

Occupational therapist.

(ok-yuh-pay'-shun-al ther'-uh-pist)

An occupational therapist helps patients recover their maximum psychological and physical function after illness, injury, or disability by using creative activities like crafts and painting for therapeutic treatment (a treatment to help a patient get well).

Oncologist.

(on-kol'-oh-jist)

This specialist studies, diagnoses, and treats all types of cancer, as well as other malignant (cancerous) or benign (non-cancerous) tumors.

Ophthalmologist.

(of-thal-moll'-oh-jist)

An ophthalmologist studies, diagnoses, and medically or surgically treats all eye disease, injuries to the eye, and vision problems.

Optician.

(op-tish'-an)

An optician makes and sells eyeglasses and contact lenses according to the prescriptions of ophthalmologists and optometrists.

Optometrist.

(op-tom'-eh-trist)

This licensed professional examines eyes for vision defects and eye disorders and prescribes corrective lenses (eyeglasses or contact lenses), as well as other treatments that do not require prescription medications or surgical procedures. The patient is referred to an ophthalmologist if medicines or surgery are needed.

Oral and maxillofacial surgeon.

(ohr'-ahl and mak'-sill-oh-fay-shuhl sur'-jun)

This dentist is skilled in extracting (pulling) teeth, in performing complex procedures like removing impacted wisdom teeth (teeth that are so tightly packed in their sockets that they cannot break through the gum) or a broken root, as well as in surgery of the mouth, jaw, and tempromandibular joint (hinge joint formed by the lower jaw and the temporal bone near the temple), and cosmetic surgery (to improve appearance).

Oral pathologist.

(ohr'-ahl pah-thol'-oh-jist)

This dentist diagnoses oral (mouth) diseases through biopsy (the microscopic study of living tissue specimens) and other laboratory tests. An oral pathologist is often called in by the general dentist treating a patient with a difficult disorder.

Orthodontist.

(or-tho-don'-tist)

This dentist specializes in preventing and treating bite and jaw problems in both children and adults by applying braces.

Orthopaedic surgeon.

(or-thoh-pee'-dik sur'-jun)

An orthopaedic surgeon (or specialist in orthopaedics) medically and surgically treats disorders, diseases, deformities, and fractures of the bones, joints, ligaments (strong, band-like connective tissue that connects bones and holds the organs in place), and muscles of the arms, legs, spine, hips, knees, feet, shoulders, elbows, and hands.

Osteopath.

(os'-tih-oh-path)

A doctor of osteopathic medicine (D.O.) focuses on the whole person (mind and body) rather than on a particular disease or disorder of a certain part of the body. Treatments used are manipulation of muscles and bones, palpation (examination by touch). The patient's diet and environment are considered in order to diagnose, treat, and maintain health. Osteopaths are licensed doctors, mostly in general practice. Some specialize in psychiatry, cardiology, surgery, pediatrics, and other medical specialties. The difference between medical doctors and osteopaths is in the way they diagnose and treat patients.

Otolaryngologist.

(oh-toh-lar-ing-gol'-oh-jist)

Also known as an ENT specialist, the otolaryngologist studies, diagnoses, and treats diseases, disorders, and injuries of the ears, nose, and throat.

Otologist.

(oh-tol'-uh-jist)

This doctor specializes in studying, diagnosing and medically or surgically treating ear diseases.

Pain management specialist.

(payn man'-ij-ment spesh'-uh-list)

This doctor treats patients with acute or chronic pain, and often consults with the family practitioner or other specialists.

Paramedic.

(par-uh-med-ik')

In the absence of a medical doctor, this specially trained professional gives first aid or emergency care.

Pathologist.

(paa-thol'-oh-jist)

A pathologist studies, diagnoses, and monitors the nature, development, and result of disease by collecting information from laboratory tests and microscopic examination of tissue specimens, body fluids, cells, and excrement.

Pediatric allergist.

(pee-dee-at'-rik al'-er-gist)

An allergist who specializes in the diagnosis and treatment of allergies in children.

Pediatric cardiologist.

(pee-dee-at'-rik car'-dee-ahl-oh-jist)

This specialist diagnoses and treats heart disease in children.

Pediatric critical care specialist.

(pee-dee-at'-rik krit'-i-cal kare spesh'-uh-list)

A pediatric critical care specialist diagnoses and treats children with life threatening disorders such as shock and severe injury.

Pediatric emergency medicine specialist.

(pee-dee-at'-rik ee-mur'-jen-see med'-i-sin spesh'-uh-list)

This specialist treats children who need immediate care for acute illnesses and injuries.

Pediatric endocrinologist.

(pee-dee-at'-rik en-doh-kri-nol'-oh-jist)

This doctor diagnoses and treats children with chemical or hormonal disorders.

Pediatric gastroenterologist.

(pee-dee-at'-rik gas'-troh-en'-ter-ahl'-uh-jist)

This doctor diagnoses and treats children with digestive tract disorders and diseases.

Pediatric hematologist.

(pee-dee-at'-rik hee-mah-tol'-oh-jist)

This specialist treats children with blood disorders such as leukemia and anemia.

Pediatric infectious disease specialist.

(pee-dee-at'-rik in-fek-shus dih'-zeez spesh'-uh-list)

This doctor studies, diagnoses, and treats children with diseases caused by viruses, bacteria, fungus, or parasites.

Pediatric nephrologist.

(pee-dee-at'-rik neh-phrol'-uh-jist)

Children with kidney disorders are diagnosed and treated by this specialist.

Pediatric nurse practitioner.

(pee-dee-at'-rik nurs prak-tish'-uh-ner)

This registered nurse specializes in providing nursing care to children.

Pediatric oncologist.

(pee-dee-at'-rik on-kol'-oh-jist)

Children with cancer are diagnosed and treated by a pediatric oncologist.

Pediatric otolaryngologist.

(pee-dee-at'-rik oh-toh-lar-ing-gol'-oh-jist)

This specialist diagnoses and treats children with disorders of the ear, nose, and throat.

Pediatric pathologist.

(pee-dee-at'-rik pa-thol-oh-jist)

A pediatric pathologist diagnoses and monitors disease in children by gathering information on their disorders from laboratory tests and microscopic examination of tissue, cells, and body fluids.

Pediatric pulmonary specialist.

(pee-dee-at'-rik pull'-moh-nar-ee spesh'-uh-list)

Children with respiratory disease involving the lungs and chest are diagnosed and treated by this specialist.

Pediatric rheumatologist.

(pee-dee-at'-rik roo-muh-tol'-uh-jist)

A pediatric rheumatologist diagnoses and treats children with diseases of the joints, muscles, bones, and tendons.

Pediatric sports medicine specialist.

(pee-dee-at'-rik spohrts med'--i-sin spesh'-uh-list)

This doctor diagnoses and treats children with bone, muscle, tendon, and ligament injuries suffered as the result of athletic activity.

Pediatric surgeon.

(pee-dee-at'-rik sur'-jun)

A pediatric surgeon surgically treats children with disease, deformity, or injury.

Pediatrician.

(pee-dee-ah-trish'-an)

A pediatrician provides general health care to children from birth to adolescence. This doctor diagnoses, evaluates, and treats developmental problems, diseases, and illnesses, and provides preventive care like checkups and vaccinations.

Pedodontist.

(peh-doh-don'-tist)

A pedodontist is a dentist with special training in treating children. This specialist evaluates the emotional and psychological effects of a patient's treatment, especially when the dental problem is complicated.

Periodontist.

(per-i-oh-don'-tist)

This dentist specializes in studying and treating problems of the gum, connecting tissue, and the bones that surround and support the teeth.

Pharmacist.

(far'-mah-sist)

Also called a druggist (drug'-ist), this person is licensed to prepare and dispense drugs according to a doctor's prescription.

Physiatrist.

(fizz-eye'-uh-trist)

A physiatrist specializes in physical medicine and rehabilitation. This doctor diagnoses, evaluates, and treats disorders and disabilities of the musculoskeletal, neurologic, and cardiovascular systems and prescribes therapeutic exercise, the application of heat or cold, the use of electrical devices, orthotics (support devices like braces), prosthetics (devices like artificial limbs to replace missing parts of the body), and prescription drugs to relieve pain and restore as much physical, psychological, social, and vocational function to the patient as possible.

Physical therapist.

(fizz'-i-kal ther'-uh-pist)

A physical therapist is trained to help rehabilitate patients with disorders and injuries that involve the muscles, joints, bones, and nerves by using such therapies as heat, cold, electrical stimulation, ultrasound, and exercises. The therapy (treatment) provided is prescribed by a physiatrist or sports medicine specialist.

Physician assistant.

(fi-zish'-en ah-sis'-tant)

This trained and certified professional performs some of the functions of a medical doctor (M.D.), including a variety of clinical procedures, under the doctor's supervision.

Plastic and reconstructive surgeon.

(plas'-tik and ree-kun-struk'-tiv sur'-jun)

This doctor evaluates and surgically treats patients with abnormal body structures, developmental or congenital (existing at the time of birth) defects, and deformities caused by infection, trauma, or tumor in order to repair, reconstruct, or improve physical defects of the skin, the musculoskeletal system, the head and face, and other parts of the body. This surgery is performed to both improve the patient's appearance and to improve his or her ability to function.

Podiatrist.

(puh-di'-uh-trist)

A podiatrist earns a doctor of podiatric medicine (D.P.N.) degree which allows this professional to medically and surgically treat foot disorders such as corns (a rough growth of thick tissue with a tender core that forms over a bone because of friction or pressure), bunions (inflamation and enlargement of the big toe joint), bone spurs (an abnormal boney growth), warts (small and occasionally hard skin growth usually caused by a virus), tumors (abnormal growths of cells), foot and toe deformities, and fractures.

Preventive medicine specialist.

(pri-ven'-tiv med'-i-sin spesh'-uh-list)

A preventive medicine specialist studies the health of individuals and groups of people to prevent disease, disability, and early death. This doctor promotes and maintains people's health by immunization, teaching good health practices, and studying environmental and occupational safety, as well as investigating the causes of epidemics and acute and chronic illnesses. A preventive medicine specialist is usually associated with public and occupational health agencies, managed care systems, or aviation and space agencies.

Prosthodontist.

(pross'-theh-don'-tist)

This dentist specializes in the replacement of missing teeth with artificial ones, caps, bridges, or dentures. General dentists refer patients with cases they are not expert in dealing with to a prosthodontist.

Psychiatric and mental health nurse.
(sy-kee-at'-trik and men'-tul helth nurs)

This registered nurse cares for patients with mental and emotional disorders.

Psychiatrist.
(sy-ky'-eh-trist)

A psychiatrist specializes in diagnosing, treating, and preventing mental illnesses, emotional disorders, and addiction to drugs or other substances like foods, alcohol, and cigarettes. The treatment includes psychoanalysis, prescription drugs, or both.

Psychic healer.
(sy'-kik heel'-er)

The psychic, or spiritual healer emphasizes the positive side of illness by focusing on comfort, hope, spiritual cleansing, and life after death. Disease, and other forms of illness, are overcome through spiritual healing even if the person dies. Edgar Cayce, the most famous psychic healer, entered self-induced trances in which illnesses were diagnosed and remedies prescribed. Treatments include exercise, diet, massage, castor oil packs, spinal manipulation, herbal teas, homeopathic medicines, special cosmetics and shampoos, enemas, and fasting. The psychic healer is not recognized by the medical community.

Psychologist.

(sy-kol'-oh-jist)

A psychologist, a specialist in the science of the mind and how it works, analyzes and treats people with mental and emotional problems with counseling therapy. A psychologist is not a medical doctor and cannot prescribe drugs.

Public health dental specialist.

(pub'-lik helth den'-tul spesh'-uh-list)

This dentist specializes in community dental health education, community and school screening programs, and floridation issues.

Pulmonary specialist.

(pull'moh-nar-ee spesh'-uh-list)

This doctor diagnoses and treats lung and chest disorders and diseases, such as pneumonia, pleurisy, bronchitis, emphysema, sleep disorders, occupational diseases, and cancer.

Radiologist.

(ray-dee-ahl'-uh-jist)

A radiologist is a doctor who uses different types of radiation, such as x-ray, as well as nonradioactive equipment, like ultrasound and magnetic resonance imaging (MRI), to diagnose and treat disease.

Reflexologist.

(ree'-flek-sol'-eh-jist)

This person relies on a map of the various parts of the body as they correspond to various reflex points on the feet to determine the condition of organs, or body systems. The appropriate points are then manipulated by massage-- applying pressure using the fingers, thumbs, combs, rubber bands, or roller massagers. This treatment supposedly cures many illnesses and injuries--from arthritis to sore throats. While reflexology treatments might be relaxing, they are otherwise bunk.

Registered nurse.

(rej'-i-stird nurs)

A registered nurse has completed the educational requirements for a state license needed to provide general and specialized nursing care.

Resident.

(rez'-i-dent)

A resident is a doctor who works for a hospital while training for certification in a particular specialty.

Rheumatologist.

(roo-muh-tol'-uh-jist)

This doctor studies, diagnoses and treats diseases of the joints, muscles, bones, and tendons, such as arthritis, rheumatism, muscle strains, and back pain.

Social worker.

(soh'-shul wur'-ker)

This person works with sick, elderly, disabled, and handicapped people both in and out of the hospital. A social worker helps them cope with their health problems and such related problems as home care, shopping, insurance, housing, environment, family care, and transportation.

Sports medicine specialist.

(spohrts med'i-sin spesh'-uh-list)

This doctor specializes in preventing injury and disease and maintaining patient health and fitness. A sports medicine specialist also treats injuries and illnesses caused by sports and athletic activities.

Therapeutic touch practitioner.

(ther'-uh-pyoo-tik tuch prak-tish'-uh-ner)

This person uses a modern version of the spiritual practice of laying on of hands. Therapeutic touch is supposedly a way of detecting illness in a person, locating the point of pain, and stimulating the patient's energy field to focus on recuperation. A registered nurse (Dolores Krieger) introduced therapeutic touch into nurses training programs and hospitals as a way of relieving a patient's pain through relaxation so the healing process can begin.

Thoracic surgeon.

(thoh-rass'-ik sur'jun)

This doctor surgically treats heart, lung, and chest area disorders, such as coronary artery disease, chest wall, lung, and esophagus (a muscular tube that connects the mouth to the stomach) cancers, heart valve and great vessel (major blood vessels) abnormalities, congenital (exisiting from birth) disorders, and chest and airway injuries.

Urologist.

(yuh-rol'-uh-jist)

A urologist studies, diagnoses, and medically or surgically treats benign (non-cancerous) or malignant (cancerous) disorders of the adrenal gland (the gland that increases the body's rate of metabolism and prepares it for stress), urinary tract, bladder, and the male genitourinary system (genital and urinary organs).

Vascular surgeon.

(vass'-kyuh-lur sur'-jun)

This specialist surgically treats disorders that affect the blood vessels, except those of the heart, lungs, and brain.

The Doctors and Other Health Care Givers Listed by Subject

Abdominal surgery.

abdominal surgeon,17

Acute illness

critical care specialist, 28

critical care surgeon, 28

emergency medicine specialist, 30

paramedic, 51

Acupressure.

chiropractor, 25

Acupuncture.

acupuncturist, 17

Addiction.

adolescent psychiatrist, 18

psychiatrist, 61

Chemicals and hormones.

Children.

orthodontist, 48

pedodontist, 56

periodontist, 57

prosthodontist, 60-1

public health dental specialist, 63

Diet and nutrition.

allergist, 19

family physician, 32

gastroenterologist, 32-3

nutritionist, 44

pediatric allergist, 51

pediatric gastroenterologist, 53

Digestive system.

abdominal surgeon, 17

colon and rectal surgeon, 27

gastroenterologist, 32-3

pediatric gastroenterologist, 53

Disease research.

clinical and laboratory immunology specialist, 26

hematologist, 35

Doctors.

radiologist, 63

resident, 65

rheumatologist, 65

sports medicine specialist, 66

thoracic surgeon, 67

urologist, 67

vascular surgeon, 68

Ears.

audiologist, 22

family physician, 32

otolaryngologist, 50

otologist, 50

pediatric otolaryngologist, 54

Elderly people.

family physician, 32

geriatric psychiatrist, 33

geriatrician, 33-4

social worker, 65

Emergency medicine.

critical care specialist, 28

critical care surgeon, 28

emergency medicine specialist, 52

paramedic, 51

pediatric critical care specialist, 52

pediatric emergency medicine specialist, 52

Endocrine system.

endocrinologist, 31

pediatric endocrinologist, 52

Environmental health and illness.

clinical ecology practitioner, 26-7

preventive medicine specialist, 60

Excretory system.

colon and rectal surgeon, 27

gastroenterologist, 32-3

nephrologist, 43

pediatric gastroenterologist, 53

pediatric nephrologist, 53

urologist, 67

Eyes.

family physician, 32

Hearing.

Heart.

Herbal remedies.

Homeopathy.

homeopathist, 37-8

Hormones.

endocrinologist, 31

gynecologist, 34

pediatric endocrinologist, 52

urologist, 67

Infant care.

neonatal-perinatal medicine specialist, 42

pediatrician, 56

Infectious disease.

immunologist, 38

infectious disease specialist, 39

pediatric infectious disease specialist, 53

preventive medicine specialist, 60

Internal systems.

cardiologist, 22

endocrinologist, 31

family physician, 32

gastroenterologist, 32-3

therapeutic touch practitioner, 66

Lungs.

pediatric pulmonary specialist, 55

pulmonary specialist, 63

thoracic surgeon, 67

Midwifery.

certified nurse-midwife, 23

Mind.

adolescent psychiatrist, 18

child psychiatrist, 24

child psychologist, 24

geriatric psychiatrist, 33

psychiatric and mental health nurse, 61

psychiatrist, 61

psychologist, 62

Mouth.

dentist (general dentistry), 29-30

endodontist, 31

oral and maxillofacial surgeon, 47

oral pathologist, 48

Nervous system.

Nose.

Nurses.

pathologist, 51

pediatric pathologist, 54-5

Physician assistance.

physician assistant, 58

See also **Nurses**

Pregnancy and birth.

certified nurse-midwife, 23

maternal gynocological neonatal nurse, 41

neonatal-perinatal medicine specialist, 42

obstetrician, 45

Prescription drugs.

pharmacist, 57

Psychic healing.

psychic healer, 61-2

Public health.

preventive medicine specialist, 60

public health dental specialist, 63

Rectum.

colon and rectal surgeon, 27

gastroenterologist, 32-3

oral and maxillofacial surgeon, 47

orthopaedic surgeon, 48-9

pediatric surgeon, 56

plastic and reconstructive surgeon, 59

urologist, 67

vascular surgeon, 68

Teeth.

dental hygenist, 29

dental technician, 29

dentist (general dentistry), 29-30

endodontist, 31

oral and maxillofacial surgeon, 47

oral pathologist, 48

orthodontist, 48

pedodontist, 56

periodontist, 57

prosthodontist, 60-1

Therapeutic touch.

therapeutic touch practitioner, 66

Throat.

Selected Bibiography: Health, Medicine, and the Human Body

Adderly, Brenda D. *The Complete Guide to Nutritional Supplements: Everything You Need to Make Informed Choices for Optimum Health*. Los Angeles: NewStar, 1998. *American Dental Directory*. Chicago: American Dental Association, 1998.

Bantam Medical Dictionary. Prepared by the editors of Market House Books. New York: Bantam, 1990.

Bruce, Debra Fulghum, with Harris H. McIlwain. *The Unofficial Guide to Alternative Medicine*. New York: Macmillan, 1998.

Cambridge Illustrated History of Medicine. Roy Porter, ed. New York, Cambridge University Press, 1996.

Compact American Medical Dictionary: A Concise and Up-to-Date Guide to Medical Terms. Boston:

Houghton Mifflin, 1998.

Complete Family Guide to Alternative Medicine: An Illustrated Encyclopedia of Natural Healing. C. Norman Shealy, ed. Rockport, MA: Element Books, 1996.

Dennerll, Jean Tannis. *Medical Terminology Made Easy.* Albany, NY: Delmar, 1998.

Drug and Natural Medicine Advisor: The Complete Guide to Alternative and Conventional Medications. New York: Time-Life, 1997.

Gray, Henry. *Anatomy: Descriptive and Surgical.* T. Pickering Pick, and Robert Howden, eds. 15th ed. New York: Barnes & Noble. 1995.

Hunt, Morton M. *The Story of Psychology.* New York: Doubleday, 1993.

Johns Hopkins Family Health Book. By Johns Hopkins University. New York: Harper Collins, 1999.

Johns Hopkins Symptoms and Remedies: The Complete Home Remedy Medical Reference. Simeon Margolis, med. ed. Prepared by the editors of Johns Hopkins Medical Letter Health After 50. rev. and updated new ed. New York:

Rebus, 1999.

Know Your Body: The Atlas of Anatomy. Berkeley, CA: Ulysses

Press, 1999.

Marieb, Elaine M. *Essentials of Human Anatomy & Physiology.*

6th ed. San Francisco: Benjamin/Cummings Science

Publishing, 1999.

Mayo Clinic Family Health Book. 2nd ed. David E. Larson,

editor-in-chief. New York: William Morrow, 1996.

Merck Manual of Medical Information. Home Edition.

Whitehouse Station, NJ: Merck Research Laboratories,

1997.

Official ABMS Directory of Board Certified Medical Specialists.

31st ed. New Providence, NJ: Marquis Who's Who,

1998.

Oxford Companion to the Mind. Richard L. Gregory, ed. New

York: Oxford University Press, 1998.

PDR Family Guide: Encyclopedia of Medical Care. New York:

Three Rivers Press, 1997.

PDR Family Guide to Natural Medicines and Healing

Therapies. New York: Three Rivers Press, 1999.

PDR Pocket Guide to Prescription Drugs. 3rd ed. rev. and
updated. New York: Pocket Books, 1998.

Physician's Desk Reference. Montvale, NJ: Medical Economics,
annual.

Rosenfeld, Isadore. *Dr. Rosenfeld's Guide to Alternative
Medicine: What Works, What Doesn't--and What's
Right for You.* New York: Fawcett Columbine, 1996.

Sharp, Vicki F. and Richard M. Sharp. *WebDoctor:Finding the
Best Health Care Online.* New York: St. Martin's
Griffin, 1998.

*Symptoms--Their Causes and Cures: How to Understand and
Treat 265 Health Concerns.* By the editors of Prevention
Magazine Health Books. Alice Feinstein, ed. New York:
Bantam, 1996.

Total Nutrition: The Only Guide You'll Ever Need. Victor
Herbert and Genell J. Subak-Sharpe, eds. New York: St.
Martin's Griffin, 1995.

Ulene, Art. *The NutriBase Nutrition Facts Desk Reference: The*

Single Encyclopedic Source for the Most Complete, Up-to-Date, and Comprehensive Collection of Food Values. Garden City Park, NY: Avery Publishing Group, 1995.

About the Author

Rosemarie Riechel received her MLS and Ph.D. from Columbia University School of Library Service, and was the reference and online specialist in the Queens Borough Public Library system for many years. She is presently an independent writer and researcher. She has published many titles about reference service in libraries.

www.ingramcontent.com/pod-product-compliance
Lightning Source LLC
Chambersburg PA
CBHW050359290526
45786CB00003B/1048